5·30·75

Dave and Diane,

May you always
be " Very Married "

Theresa & Bob Eubanks

Love Poems for the Very Married

By Lois Wyse
The Compleat Child (with Joan Javits)
Help! I Am the Mother of a Teen-Age Girl
P.S. Happy Anniversary
Two Guppies, a Turtle, and Aunt Edna
What Kind of a Girl Are You, Anyway?

Love Poems for the Very Married

Lois Wyse

WORLD PUBLISHING

TIMES MIRROR

NEW YORK

Published by The World Publishing Company
Published simultaneously in Canada
by Nelson, Foster & Scott Ltd.
Fifteenth printing—1972
Copyright © 1967 by Lois Wyse
All rights reserved
ISBN 0-529-04050-6
Library of Congress catalog card number: 67-12080
Printed in the United States of America

WORLD PUBLISHING
TIMES MIRROR

For my love
with my love

Contents

I Think I Love You

Once, when we were very young,
You looked at me and said,
"I think I love you."
And I bristled slightly
(as young girls do).
And I said to you, "Think?
You only think you love me?
You mean you do not know?"

For at that moment I knew love.
I was on intimate terms with Cole Porter lyrics,
And I cried when I read Wuthering Heights.

But now that I have grown up
I know the timeless treasure of your words.
For love must have a way to grow,
And you found the way so long ago.
You took the time to think our love...
And still you do.
A good love takes thinking through.
And living with.
And I knew
The first morning I awoke and touched you next to me . . .
I, too, could say,
"I think I love you."

A Cozy Heart

Once I thought that love
Was tempestuous,
Tumultuous,
"Kiss me quick."

I was wrong.

Love is usually a very comfortable way of life,
A cozy heart,
Kisses on the cheek,
"Wear your rubbers and blow your nose."

And what keeps a love so cozy?
The fact that every so often love is
Tempestuous, tumultuous . . .
"Kiss me quick."

Heart-to-Heart

There is a cord
Unseen
That binds us heart-to-heart.
The surest way
For me to shorten the cord
Is to let you choose the length.

For if I choose to tighten
That unseen cord
By poking,
Prying,
Wondering,
Why?-ing,
You will dissolve the cord
And create
An unseen wall
For both of us to see.

And that, my beloved,
Would be the tragedy
Of this
Or any
Marriage.

Nothing

I suppose it was something you said
That caused me to tighten
And pull away.
And when you asked,
"What is it?"
I, of course, said,
"Nothing."

Whenever I say, "Nothing,"
You may be very certain there is something.
The something is a cold, hard lump of
Nothing.

Zipped

How many times have you stood in the doorway
And watched while I
Zipped,
Gartered,
Fastened,
Buttoned,
Combed,
Mascaraed,
Tugged and pulled at
Me?

I do not know, my love.
I do not know how many times.
But please, my sweet, don't ever turn your head.

Possessed

Remember once
I said to you,
"I'm not a possessive woman."
(I was wearing the white lace robe at the time.)
"I'll never try to own you."
(That night it was the pale green with black lace.)
"Darling, you're free. You're loose. You are your own man."
(The blue shift it was. The one with bows on the shoulders.)
"Dearest, of course you don't have to meet me. It's your choice."
(Pale pink, I think, with a diaphanous skirt.)
"I waited for your call, my love."
(Two bows in my hair . . . white mules on my feet.)
I know I said I'm not possessive.
And when I said it
I wasn't I wasn't I wasn't.
Now, however, I am a very possessive woman.
(And I can't remember what I'm wearing.)

Yes

"Do you still want me?" you asked.
And I said, "You don't have to ask me every day."
You said, "Well, do you?"
And I said, "Yes."

But what I really said within my heart was,
"Want him?"
Do I want him?
In an exotic, quixotic way
I want him.
I want him because
I can walk with him,
And he talks to me about the things I like to talk about.
And he says funny things to me,
And sometimes he thinks they're so funny
He says them twice.
And I know him better than
Any woman has any right to know a man.
And with all that I find
Just when I think I know him best,
I know him not at all.
And all I really want is a chance to know him better,
And that takes time.
And I would like to take all the time given me
To know him better
Which is the real reason
I cannot bear to be away from him.
"Yes."

Sec

The waiter brought the wine to the table,
And you sipped it carefully,
Nodded slightly,
And went on saying what you were saying
Which was
"I love you."

And then you said,
"Now taste the wine.
It's very good, very dry."
Oh no, it's not my
Dear.
When you said,
"I love you,"
I tasted but the sweetest wine.

The Quicker to See You Again

We reached the corner of the street,
And you turned and walked away.
But not I.
I ran.
I ran from you as quickly as I could.
I felt your eyes upon my fast-retreating back
And knew that you kept turning 'round
To watch me run away.

But what you could not know
As I ran down the street
Was that I ran because
I cannot bear to walk away from you.

Just Then

The other day
You looked at me.
You did not say,
"I love you,"
But just then you believed it.

The Grand Ballroom of the Plaza Hotel

Our marriage was not made
In a chilly chapel,
Country church or
The Grand Ballroom of the Plaza Hotel.

For it was only long after the ceremony
That we learned
Why we got married
In the first place.

The Good Life

The other night
I was involved
In a discussion
Of the good life . . .
Whatever that is:
Colony
    Balenciaga
       Firenze
Chablis
          A fireplace that works
        Chanel #5
   Two weeks in Acapulco
     Ice cream
Then someone mentioned
Love
And a man's great need for wife
Or mistress.

I moved back
Into my
Very own thoughts
And mentally echoed
The words of the speaker as he sipped his tea,
"A man's great need for wife or mistress."
And I silently said,
"Wife or mistress?
Oh, you poor man.
How sad it is you do not know
The Good Life is
One woman who is both."

Sunday

Sometimes
When we talk
I get the distinct feeling
You are not glad
You are you
I am me
And
We are we.

I detect a detached chill.

It used to worry me
Until I realized
That only a man
Who can be very attached
Can also be very detached.
And though at times I still detect detachment
I can weather it.
For I have come to learn that
You and I, my love,
Do not live in a temperate zone.

My Toes Don't Curl

When I open the door
And see you there,
I don't hear bells,
My toes don't curl,
My heart does not beat faster.

Until later.

A State of Mind?

ESP?
Do I believe in ESP?
When you asked, I laughed and said,
"ESP? I don't even believe in CIA."
So maybe it wasn't such a good joke.
But don't you see . . .
I believe in ESP so much
I'm afraid to say I do.
I believe that when you are away
You know the times I'm frightened . . .
Or why would you call just
At the moment
The frantic, unsaid call for help is sent
From my mind to yours?
Why would you say,
"At three o'clock today
I thought of you."
Does the long arm of coincidence
Have a short life?
Can you believe that you and I
Are a state of mind?

I Wish for You

I wish for you
Each small success
That makes a man a man.

I wish for you
An outside cut,
A twist of lime,
An order from the Coast,
A second look from pretty girls,
A second look for pretty girls,
And one glittering riposte.

I wish for you
Unshaven Sundays,
Brilliant Mondays,
And occasionally a day with nothing to do . . .
But ride waves or bikes or roller skates
And reflect, my dear, on
The importance of Not Being Corporate You.

Let others wish you
Hand-tailored suits,
English boots,
And dream executive dreams for you.
It is only money that they wish, my sweet,
But I want riches for you.

I Understand You Better Than You Think I Do

There they were:
The careful measured tones . . .
So clear that I could see them.
They precede always
Something important
That you will say.

So I closed my mind
And shut my ears
Because never yet have you
Said something joyous
In a
Something Important Voice.

Even now as I recall
The fragments of your thoughts
I am not sure just what you said,
But I am sure you meant
"No."

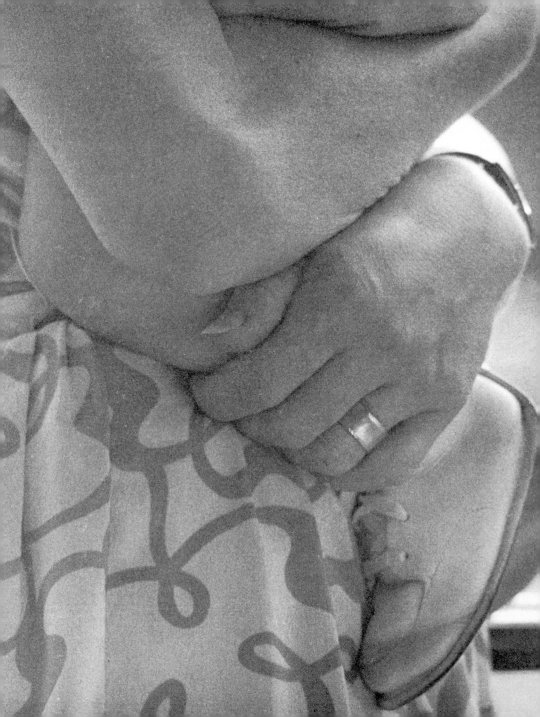

For an Out-of-Town Husband

Of course you have to travel.
All husbands have to travel,
But I thought you ought to know that
We are so married I know you by your telephone ring.
It is a short, impatient ring
Followed by a long,
"Hello how are the children did you have a good day?"
Then sometimes there is silence
Which is a very nice thing in a marriage.
And during that silence
We both say the most understanding things of all.

Half-Squeezed

Somewhere in the
Half-squeezed tube of toothpaste,
In the comb of mine
You use,
In the TV shows we lie and watch . . .
Somewhere in all of this
We sink our roots.

We draw our strength
In such strange ways.
We build our life
On toothpaste, combs, and
Television shows with highly predictable endings.

Central Park South

Sometimes when I'm not with you
I pretend I am,
And I walk through the park.
Do you know something . . .
It's really very dirty in the park.
I mean there are big old rubbish grinders
That roll down the paths
Stirring yesterday's dust all over today
And the benches aren't clean
And even the ducks look dirty.

But when I look
Across the lake
And see the rock
Where we sometimes sit,
The park looks bright once more.

Non-Stop

Someone asked me
To name the time
Our friendship stopped
And love began.

Oh, my darling,
That's the secret.
Our friendship
Never stopped.

I Just Talked to You on the Telephone

There is a certain tone
That creeps into your voice
From time to time.

Not demanding
Or impatient.
Insistent is the word,
I think.

A combination of
Male assertiveness
And possessiveness.

And I like it.

Lines to an Unhandy Man

You never made
A lamp base out of a Cracker Jack box,
An extra room out of an unused closet,
Or a garden out of a pile of clay.
All you ever made was
A woman out of me.

On Deposit in a Secret Heart

It's like money in the bank.
The delicate, off-balance, improbable things
   that happen in a moment . . .
The day you said you couldn't see me off,
Then at the last minute came to the station as the train
   was leaving
And raced the diesel along the track.
And I said, "It's just like the movies."
And you said, "Yes, it's just like the movies,"
And we kissed without ever touching.
Or the day . . . or the day . . . or the day . . .
All the delicate
Off-balance
Improbable things that happen in a moment
To be stored and treasured
On deposit in a secret heart . . .
Withdrawn when needed,
And redeposited for another rainy day.

Half Past Loving

It was very casual
And a game of sorts.
You covered the face of the clock
And told me to guess the time.
I guessed, and I was wrong.
As usual.
You guessed, and you were right.
As usual.

I didn't really know
Just what that proved
Until the day you covered the face of the clock
And guessed the time, and you were wrong.

And suddenly I knew
That made us right.

A Private Place

There is within each of us
A private place
For thinking private thoughts
And dreaming private dreams.

But in the shared experience of marriage,
Some people cannot stand the private partner.

How fortunate for me
That you have let me grow,
Think my private thoughts,
Dream my private dreams.

And bring a private me
To the shared experience of marriage.

Maybe I Unplugged the Phone

I started to write a poem to you,
And my pen ran dry.
My mouth ran dry.
My heart pounded.
"There is terrible significance in this,"
I thought.
I ran and found another pen
And wrote . . .
Not easily . . .
But I wrote.
"See, everything is still all right,"
I said to me.

Why didn't you call from Los Angeles today?

Do You Need Me?

Remember that day in New York?
You know, the last day we were there.
I had just bought the pink suit
(the one with the funny loops you like so much).
I walked out of the store,
And I saw one of those there-on-the-sidewalk phone booths
So I called the hotel for messages.
The operator read all the usual nothings.
And then she came to that message from you.
It said, "Do you need me? I'll be at . . ."
Funny.
I never heard where you'd be.
I heard only
"Do you need me?"
And I thought,
"Do I need you?"
And slowly I put the receiver back on the hook
And I said to myself . . .
Oh, how I need you.
This very moment I need you.
How dear you are. How right that you should show me what
"I love you"
Really means.

Photographs by Gary Winogrand
Designed by Herb Lubalin & Fran Elfenbein